CLASSIC
CHRISTIANITY
STUDY
SERIES

A Closer Look at
The Truth
About Prayer

BOB GEORGE

HARVEST HOUSE PUBLISHERS
Eugene, Oregon 97402

A CLOSER LOOK AT THE TRUTH ABOUT PRAYER

Copyright © 1994 by Harvest House Publishers
Eugene, Oregon 97402

ISBN 1-56507-174-3

Printed in the United States of America.

94   95   96   97   98   99   00   —   10   9   8   7   6   5   4   3   2   1

Contents

No Other Foundation

As a person's physical growth is based on proper diet and exercise, so a Christian's spiritual growth depends on regular feeding upon the Word of God and application of its truth. With more false teaching, shifting opinions, and general confusion in the world than ever before, Christians need a solid foundation upon which to base their beliefs and build their lives. The Word of God declares that Jesus Christ is that foundation of truth. Therefore the emphasis of the Classic Christianity Study Series is in helping Christians discover for themselves what the Bible actually says about Christ.

These Bible study guides are uniquely prepared for this purpose. They are useful for the newborn, intermediate, or mature Christian in that they begin with the fundamental and central question of who Jesus Christ is and then build upon that foundation in a logical and progressive manner. The Classic Christianity Study Series is also extremely flexible in that it can be used for individual or group study.

The book of Acts tells us that the first Christians were "continually devoting themselves to the apostles' *teaching* and to *fellowship*, to the *breaking of bread* and to *prayer*" (Acts 2:42 NASB). The need for a proper balance in the Christian life is as real today as it was in the first century. The Classic Christianity Study Series has therefore been designed to incorporate all of these elements vital for spiritual growth.

No man can lay a foundation other than the one which is laid, which is Jesus Christ (1 Corinthians 3:11 NASB).

Helpful Suggestions
As You Begin

1. Choose a convenient time and location. This will help you to be consistent in your study.

2. Use a Bible that you are comfortable with.

3. Before beginning your study, always ask God to quiet your heart and open your mind to understand the Scriptures.

4. Approach the Word of God with a learner's heart and a teachable spirit.

1

What Is Prayer?

What is prayer? It is merely talking with God. It is intelligent, personal communication with our heavenly Father, who loves us and whom we love. Through prayer we voice our concerns and needs to God. We make our requests known to Him. Even more important, we listen to what He says to us. Prayer is an outflow of our relationship to God through Jesus Christ.

Too many of us, however, view prayer as a way to get what we want, or as a ritual to make us more spiritual. Through these views we see God either as the great vending machine or the great ogre in the sky. In both cases, prayer is reduced to a formula we follow to approach God, rather than communicate with God as a result of our personal relationship with Him.

From Genesis through Revelation we encounter people who prayed. Sometimes their prayers are recorded for us to read, at other times the Bible simply says they prayed. Whatever the case, we see the people of the Bible constantly talking with God.

The Bible tells *us* to pray as well. However, as we read through its pages, what we see more than the *command* to pray is the *assumption* that we will pray. This testifies to the need in the heart of every one of us to know God and communicate with Him.

But we want to know how to pray. We ask, "When and how should I pray? Should I pray on my knees, or sitting, or standing? Should I pray in public, or should I pray in private? Should I pray persistently about something, or should I ask God just once and trust Him to answer?"

As we take a closer look at this subject, we will see there are no rigid rules to follow in true biblical prayer. It is simply talking and listening to your best friend, the One who lives in you, who loves you and wants the very best for you.

Key Verse: Colossians 4:2

Devote yourselves to prayer, being watchful and thankful.

---

1. What are we to devote ourselves to?

2. What attitudes does Paul say we should have in prayer?

3. Paul also told the believers in Rome to be "faithful in prayer" (Romans 12:12). In light of the above verses, what is the importance of prayer in your life?

Prayer is an important part of the believer's life. We read in the book of Acts that the early church "devoted themselves to the apostles' teaching and to the fellowship, to the breaking of bread and to prayer" (Acts 2:42). We see throughout the four Gospels that Jesus was devoted to prayer. He was constantly communicating with His heavenly Father. As an introduction, let's take a closer look at the life of Jesus to catch a glimpse of the meaning of true biblical prayer.

The news about Him spread all the more, so that crowds of people came to hear Him and to be healed of their sicknesses. But Jesus often withdrew to lonely places and prayed (Luke 5:15,16).

1. News spread concerning Jesus and huge crowds of people came to see Him. Why did they come?

2. Despite the crowds and the many needs of the people, what did Jesus often do?

3. Why do you suppose Jesus often withdrew to lonely places and prayed?

That evening . . . the people brought to Jesus all the sick and demon-possessed. The whole town gathered at the door, and Jesus healed many who had various diseases. He also drove out many demons, but He would not let the demons speak because they knew who He was. Very early in the morning, while it was still dark, Jesus got up, left the house and went off to a solitary place, where He prayed (Mark 1:32-35).

1. Who did the people bring to Jesus? As the whole town gathered, what did Jesus do?

2. What happened very early in the morning?

Read Luke 6:12-16 and answer the following questions:

1. Where does this verse say Jesus went to pray on one particular day?

2. How long did Jesus spend praying to God? What did He do the following day?

3. What do you suppose He was talking to His Father about the previous night?

Read Matthew 14:22-25 and answer the following questions:

1. After Jesus dismissed the crowd, where did He go and for what purpose?

2. As in the other verses we have studied so far, this verse says Jesus went up on the mountainside by Himself to pray. Why do you suppose He went alone?

3. What does this tell us about His relationship with His heavenly Father?

> *Jesus looked up and said, "Father, I thank You that You have heard Me. I knew that You always hear Me, but I said this for the benefit of the people standing here, that they may believe that You sent Me." When He had said this, Jesus called in a loud voice, "Lazarus, come out!"* (John 11:41-43).

1. What did Jesus thank His Father for?

2. Did Jesus know His Father always heard Him when He prayed?

3. What does this indicate about His relationship to His Father?

4. For whose benefit was this prayer of thanksgiving?

5. What did Jesus want the people to believe concerning Him?

6. After He thanked the Father, what did He do?

7. What do you suppose Jesus prayed for?

Read John 11:21,22 and answer the following questions:

1. Martha knew that Jesus could have prevented her brother's death if He had been there. What else did she know about Jesus?

2. How do you think she knew God would give Jesus whatever He asked?

3. What does this tell us about Jesus' relationship to His Father?

The Lord's Prayer

Many people call the prayer that Jesus taught His disciples to pray (as recorded in Matthew 6) "the Lord's Prayer." However, the true Lord's Prayer is recorded in John 17. There we see the heart of true biblical prayer.

Read John 17:1-5 and answer the following questions:

1. What was Jesus' request of His Father?

2. Why did He desire to be glorified?

3. God granted Jesus authority over all people. What was this authority and how did Jesus define "eternal life"?

4. How did Jesus bring glory to His Father while here on earth?

Read John 17:6-19 and answer the following questions:

1. In these verses Jesus shifts His focus of attention to the disciples. What did Jesus say His job was concerning the disciples (verses 6-8)?

2. As a result, how did the disciples respond and what did they know for sure about Jesus (verses 6-8)?

3. In verse 9, Jesus makes the point that He is praying just for His disciples. What reason does He give for specifically praying for them?

4. What did Jesus ask His Father to do for the disciples (verses 11,15) and why (verses 13,14)?

5. Through what means did Jesus ask His Father to protect them (verses 11, 16-19)?

6. As you read Jesus' requests concerning the disciples, whose desires do you suppose Jesus' words reflect?

7. How do these verses show prayer is an outflow of our relationship to God?

Read John 17:20-26 and answer the following questions:

1. In these verses, who does Jesus pray for?

2. What was His prayer for those who have believed in Christ through the message of the disciples (verses 21,23)?

3. Our unity and oneness with Christ will let the world know what concerning God and His love for mankind (verses 21,23)?

4. What was Jesus' desire for those whom the Father had given Him (verse 24)?

5. Why did Jesus say He would continue making the Father known (verses 25,26)?

6. What does John 17 teach you about prayer?

Throughout Jesus' life He prayed to His heavenly Father—not out of obligation, but as an outflow of His relationship with His Father. This is what the Lord wants to teach *us* about prayer.

2

Our Basis for Prayer

Before we can look at the *specifics* of prayer, we need to first understand our *basis* for prayer. What gives us the ability or even the right to go to God in prayer? How was this accomplished? The answers to these questions form the foundation for properly understanding how and why we pray.

Because of Christ's death, burial, and resurrection, we have been adopted into God's family. As God's children we can boldly go before our heavenly Father and ask Him anything we like. God sees us as righteous and holy through the finished work of His Son. Let's take a closer look at the basis for prayer.

Key Verse: Hebrews 4:16

Let us then approach the throne of grace with confidence, so that we may receive mercy and find grace to help us in our time of need.

1. How is God's throne described? What does this tell us about the nature of God?

2. How are we to approach Him?

3. Does this verse say we can go to God only after we've "cleaned ourselves up"? When can we go to Him?

4. What will we find when we go to God in prayer?

During the presidency of John F. Kennedy, *Life* magazine published a photograph that is a perfect illustration of what it means to go boldly to the throne of grace. The picture was taken during the Cuban missile crisis. This was the closest the world had ever come to a nuclear war. President Kennedy was meeting with three of his top advisers in the Oval Office about the crisis. The most powerful man in the world was making decisions during one of the most critical times in history. Yet right there playing on the floor with a big smile on his face was little "John John." How did he get there?

Didn't he know he had just barged in on a very important meaning? Didn't he know that the world was on the brink of nuclear war? Obviously, the answer is no. All he knew was that the President was his daddy and he was welcome to be with him anytime he wanted to because of that fact.

Likewise, as God's children, we have an intimate relationship with our Father. He is never too busy for us. His love and acceptance of us is not based on how good we are or how well we perform.

The Finished Work of Christ

> *Therefore, brothers, since we have confidence to enter the Most Holy Place by the blood of Jesus, by a new and living way opened for us through the curtain, that is, His body, and since we have a great priest over the house of God, let us draw near to God with a sincere heart in full assurance of faith, having our hearts sprinkled to cleanse us from a guilty conscience and having our bodies washed with pure water* (Hebrews 10:19-22).

1. What attitude should we have when entering the "Most Holy Place"?

2. Who opened the way for us?

3. How did Jesus do this?

4. Who is our Great High Priest?

5. How can we draw near to God?

6. What enables us to draw near with a sincere heart in full assurance of faith?

7. Could we draw near to God apart from having our guilty conscience cleansed?

8. Why is it important to understand the work of Christ on the cross in regard to prayer?

Read Colossians 1:21,22 and answer the following questions:

1. What relationship did we have with God before we were born again?

2. Where were we enemies with God?

3. Was this alienation on God's part or our own?

4. What caused these feelings of alienation?

5. How does He see us now as His children? Can we be accused of anything?

6. Therefore, where do feelings of being alienated from God come from? Are they based on truth?

7. If we truly believed that God sees us as holy, without blemish and free from accusation, would we ever be afraid to pray?

Read 2 Corinthians 5:21 and answer the following questions:

1. Who never had any sin?

2. What did He become for us? As a result, what were we given?

3. Can we improve on this? Therefore, how acceptable are we to God?

> *By one offering He has perfected for all time those who are sanctified* (Hebrews 10:14 NASB).

1. What is the offering referred to in this verse?

2. What is the result of that offering? For how long?

3. If God has perfected you for all time, can you ever be imperfect in His sight?

4. How should knowing this change the way we approach prayer?

> *. . . and be found in Him, not having a righteousness of my own that comes from the law, but that which is through faith in Christ—the righteousness that comes from God and is by faith* (Philippians 3:9).

1. Is there any true righteousness in ourselves? Can we gain righteousness through observing the law?

2. What is the only way we can receive righteousness? What is the source of this righteousness?

3. If we have the righteousness of God through faith in Jesus Christ, how righteous are we?

The Believer's Identity in Christ

To all who received Him, to those who believed in His name, He gave the right to become children of God (John 1:12).

1. What does it mean to "receive Him"?

2. What did He give to people who believed on His name, and to how many?

3. If you have received Christ, what is your relationship to God?

4. How then should we communicate with Him?

Read Romans 8:15,16 and answer the following questions. Keep in mind that the word "abba" is a Hebrew term of endearment for a father. It translates "daddy."

1. Does a spirit of fear come from God?

2. What Spirit did we receive from God?

3. The term "abba" implies what kind of relationship?

4. What does the Spirit testify with our spirits?

> *Until now you have not asked for anything in My name. Ask and you will receive, and your joy will be complete* (John 16:24).

1. In whose name are we to pray? What will be the result?

2. How will this make our joy complete?

3. Based on the above verses, what do you think it means to pray in Jesus' name?

Jesus told us to pray in His name. So, we tack the phrase "in Jesus' name" to the end of our prayers, like "Roger. Over and out." But that phrase is actually the source of our confidence in speaking to our Father, and it expresses a vital attitude. It is the expression of our own knowledge that we have no righteousness of our own by which we can approach a holy God, but that Jesus Christ has given us His righteousness. Therefore, "In Him and through faith in Him we may approach God with freedom and confidence" (Ephesians 3:12). That is the promise we are claiming when we pray in Jesus' name.

The purpose for which Christ redeemed us is to give us a personal relationship with God. Because of His finished work on the cross, His death, and His resurrection, we can approach our heavenly Father. This is the basis for prayer.

3

What Prayer Is Not

Key Verse: Luke 11:1

One day Jesus was praying in a certain place. When He finished, one of His disciples said to Him, "Lord, teach us to pray, just as John taught his disciples."

---

1. According to the above key verse, what had Jesus just finished doing when the disciple asked Him the question?

2. Why do you think he asked Him at this particular time?

3. What relationship did Jesus have with His Father while He was on the earth?

4. What should our relationship be with the Father?

5. Is the disciple's question one that you have asked?

The disciple's question showed where his heart was. He didn't want to *get* something from God; he wanted to *learn* something from God. In other words, he was saying to Jesus, "I know the traditions of praying and the right formulas, but I want to know what the real thing is. I want to know how to have a meaningful relationship with God like You do." He was tired of empty words and vain repetitions. He wanted to learn about true prayer.

To properly understand what prayer is all about, we must first understand what prayer is not.

Read Matthew 6:5,6 and answer the following questions:

1. How did the hypocrites pray, according to this passage?

2. Why did they pray this way? What was their reward?

3. What does this reveal about their understanding of prayer?

4. How did Jesus instruct us to pray in these verses?

5. What does Jesus say the Father will do for those who pray in secret?

6. Is God concerned so much with public prayer as He is with us just talking to Him in private?

7. What does this tell us about the nature of our relationship to God?

8. In contrast to what the hypocrites understood about prayer, what can you conclude about prayer?

When you pray, do not keep on babbling like pagans, for they think they will be heard because of their many words. Do not be like them, for your Father knows what you need before you ask Him (Matthew 6:7,8).

1. Jesus warned against praying like the pagans. How did they pray?

2. Do you believe God is concerned with how long we pray or how many words we use?

3. What do pagans think it takes to get God to hear their prayers?

4. In what ways have we adopted this same attitude?

5. When we begin to use the same words over and over again, what happens to our attitude in prayer?

6. What is our view of God if it takes using many words to get Him to hear us?

7. If God knows what we need before we ask Him, do we have to do something special for Him to hear us?

8. What does this show us about God's love?

9. In light of these passages, sum up what Jesus was teaching us about prayer.

To many people, prayer is a way to relieve guilt. By constantly asking God to forgive them of their sins, they demonstrate a misunderstanding of Christ's finished work on the cross. Prayer should never be motivated by guilt or as a way to keep "short accounts" with God. Consider the following verses.

In Him we have redemption through His blood, the forgiveness of sins, in accordance with the riches of God's grace (Ephesians 1:7).

1. Where is redemption found?

2. Why wouldn't you ask God to redeem you every day?

3. Where is forgiveness found?

4. If both redemption and forgiveness are in Christ and Christ lives in you, why would you ask God to forgive you daily?

5. What are redemption and forgiveness in accordance with?

There is no fear in love. But perfect love drives out fear, because fear has to do with punishment. The one who fears is not made perfect in love (1 John 4:18).

1. What does perfect love drive out?

2. In contrast, what does fear drive out?

3. What does fear have to do with?

4. When someone is fearful, what does he think God is going to do to him?

5. Can someone be fearful of God and be experiencing His perfect love at the same time?

6. What then can you conclude about someone who prays out of a motivation of fear?

Prevalent today is the "name-it-and-claim-it" doctrine. In other words, whatever you want, just tell God and He is obligated to do it. By using certain words and formulas, you can get God to do anything you want Him to. Obviously, this is not biblical prayer, but what does the Bible teach about this?

> *Godliness with contentment is great gain. For we brought nothing into the world, and we can take nothing out of it. But if we have food and clothing, we will be content with that* (1 Timothy 6:6-8).

1. What does God consider great gain?

2. What did we bring into this world?

3. What can we take with us when we die?

4. What are the only two physical things we need?

5. Is it possible to be content with what you have and be asking for more material things at the same time?

6. Can material things bring contentment?

7. What can you conclude about praying to achieve financial gain?

> *When you ask, you do not receive, because you ask with wrong motives, that you may spend what you get on your pleasures* (James 4:3).

1. In this passage, is the problem that they do not ask?

2. What is God's answer when they ask?

3. What does this show about the doctrine that God will do whatever you ask Him?

4. What is God listening to—our words or our hearts?

5. If we are asking with selfish motives, should we expect to have that prayer answered?

As we have seen, prayer is not a performance, a way to manipulate God, a way to relieve guilt, or a way to get financial or material gain. God is not a vending machine where I can put in my quarter of faith and pull the knob in order to get what I want. Prayer is none of these things. From this point on, let's dispel these misunderstandings and see what God's Word has to teach us about prayer. He didn't leave us in the dark, but gave us some specifics concerning our communication with Him. Our attitude should be the same as the disciple's: "Lord, teach us to pray."

4

Prayer and the Word of God

It is interesting that God gave each of us two ears and one mouth. There are probably numerous reasons why. Perhaps we should do twice as much listening as talking! This applies to prayer as well as to human relationships. The "listening" aspect of prayer comes through the Word of God.

The Bible teaches us about the God we pray to. Apart from the testimony of the Word, we don't know whether we are praying to the God of the Bible or to a god of our own imagination. Prayer needs to be inspired by God speaking to us, which He does through His written Word.

Key Verse: John 15:7

If you remain in Me and My words remain in you, ask whatever you wish, and it will be given you.

---

1. This verse contains one of the greatest promises of the Bible. What does this verse say we can do?

2. What is the promise to those who ask whatever they wish?

3. What is our asking predicated upon?

4. Based on this verse, why do you think it is important to read the Word of God?

5. What attitude do the phrases "if you remain in Me" and "My words remain in you" imply we should have in our hearts as we pray?

6. If we are remaining in Christ and His words remain in us, whose desires will be reflected in our prayers?

7. Who will be the initiator of our prayers?

> *The prayer of a righteous man is powerful and effective. Elijah was a man just like us. He prayed earnestly that it would not rain, and it did not rain on the land for three and a half years. Again he prayed, and the heavens gave rain, and the earth produced its crops* (James 5:16-18).

1. What does James say about the prayer of a righteous man?

2. James used Elijah as an example. What did Elijah pray for, and what happened?

3. When he prayed again, what did he pray for, and what happened?

Most of us wish our prayers were as powerful as Elijah's. Can you imagine praying like he did and having the same type of results? Prayer would take on a whole new meaning. Yet Elijah was no different from us; James pointed out that fact. Elijah didn't have a special hotline to God, nor was he a special prayer warrior. His prayers were powerful and effective because they came straight from the Word of God.

Elijah didn't come up with the idea to ask God for the rain to stop and dry up the land. He was merely praying back to God what God had already said. In Deuteronomy 11:16,17 God said to the people of Israel: "Be careful, or you will be enticed to turn away and worship other gods and bow down to them. Then the Lord's anger will burn against you, and *He will shut the heavens so that it will not rain and the ground will yield no produce,* and you will soon perish from the good land the Lord is giving you." When Elijah was on the scene, Israel had turned away from the Lord and was worshiping Baal. So his prayer was a request to God to do exactly what He said He would do if Israel worshiped other gods.

Elijah prayed again for the rain to start because the Lord had said He would send rain: "After a long time, in the third year, the word of the Lord came to Elijah: 'Go and present yourself to Ahab, and I will send rain on the land'" (1 Kings 18:1). Elijah's prayers were powerful and effective because they were initiated by God through His Word. We have the same Word of God as Elijah. Our prayers can be just as powerful and effective if we will let God be the initiator through His Word. Let's take a closer look at the relationship between the Word of God and prayer.

> *Jesus answered, "It is written: 'Man does not live on bread alone, but on every word that comes from the mouth of God' "* (Matthew 4:4).

1. According to Jesus, what is necessary for man to live on besides bread?

2. What can you conclude about the importance of the Word of God for your daily life from this verse?

3. What relationship do you see the Word of God having with prayer?

Read 1 Peter 1:24,25 and answer the following questions:

1. How does Peter describe men and their glory?

2. What happens to grass and the flowers of the field?

3. Therefore, can anything of lasting value come from man and his glory?

4. In contrast, what does Peter say about the Word of the Lord?

5. What Word was preached to us and what confidence can we have in approaching God, knowing that we are standing on something that lasts forever?

> *Faith comes from hearing the message, and the message is heard through the word of Christ* (Romans 10:17).

1. Where does faith come from? How is the message heard?

2. What then must we depend upon to know that the attitude of our prayers is based on faith?

> *Sanctify them by the truth; Your word is truth* (John 17:17).

1. Jesus prayed that we would be sanctified by truth. What is truth, according to Jesus?

2. If we are going to find truth about God, man, and how we should live, where must we go?

3. The Bible tells us in numerous verses that God loves us. What would be the difference in a person's prayer who knows this truth and someone's prayer who does not know that God loves him?

4. How important is it to know truth in regard to prayer?

> *You diligently study the Scriptures because you think that by them you possess eternal life. These are the Scriptures that testify about Me, yet you refuse to come to Me to have life* (John 5:39,40).

1. In this conversation with the Pharisees, Jesus pointed out the reason they studied the Scriptures. What was this reason?

2. Who did Jesus say the Scriptures are about?

3. Why do the Scriptures point us to Jesus?

4. What did the Pharisees refuse to do?

5. As we read the Word of God today, who is it going to point us to, and why?

6. How will this change the way we pray?

The Word of God and You

Man is made up of a body, soul, and spirit. Each has specific needs that must be met. For example, the body needs food, air, and water to survive. If these needs aren't met, the body will die. The same is true for the soul and the spirit. The soul has specific needs that must be met on a soulish level and the spirit has specific needs that can only be met on a spiritual level.

Because of the fall, man is unable to discern the difference between soul and spirit. As a result, man has turned to the world to meet his spiritual needs. For example, many people get married in hopes of finding unconditional love and acceptance. However, unconditional love and acceptance is a *spiritual* need that can only be met by a *spiritual* being.

This is very important to know and understand when it comes to prayer. It doesn't make sense to ask God to meet a spiritual need through the things of this world—people, places, and things—and then get angry at God because He doesn't seem to answer. A spiritual need cannot be met on the soulish level. Because the Word of God does divide the soul from the spirit, we can discern what our true needs are and then pray accordingly.

Understanding the Basic Needs of Man

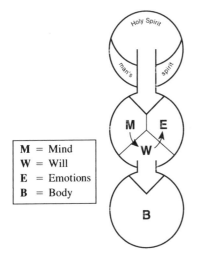

Spiritual Needs
1. Unconditional love
2. Unconditional acceptance
3. Meaning and purpose in life

Soul Needs (common to man)
1. Psychological
2. Emotional
3. Volitional

M = Mind
W = Will
E = Emotions
B = Body

Physical Needs
1. Air
2. Water
3. Food
4. Sleep
5. Clothing/shelter

The word of God is living and active. Sharper than any double-edged sword, it penetrates even to dividing soul and spirit, joints and marrow; it judges the thoughts and attitudes of the heart (Hebrews 4:12).

1. How does Peter describe the Word of God?

2. Because it is sharper than any double-edged sword, what is the Word of God able to penetrate and divide?

3. In your opinion, what is the importance of the Word of God being able to divide soul and spirit?

4. What does the Word of God judge?

5. Is it possible to pray with the wrong thoughts and motives?

6. Based on this verse, what role does the Word of God play in prayer?

All Scripture is God-breathed and is useful for teaching, rebuking, correcting and training in righteousness, so that the man of God may be thoroughly equipped for every good work (2 Timothy 3:16,17).

1. All Scripture is God-breathed and useful for what in our lives?

2. In what ways is the Word of God useful for teaching? In other words, what will we learn through the Word of God?

3. In what ways is the Word of God useful for rebuking?

4. What sort of things will the Word of God correct in our lives?

5. How will the Word of God train us in righteousness?

6. What is the end result in our lives?

7. What does this verse tell us about the sufficiency of the Word of God?

8. Based on this verse, what relationship do you see the Word of God having with prayer?

> *The Spirit gives life; the flesh counts for nothing. The words I have spoken to you are spirit and they are life* (John 6:63).

1. What does the Spirit give to us? In contrast, of what value is the flesh?

2. Of what value is prayer if it is based on the flesh?

3. What does Jesus say about the words He has spoken to us?

4. How important is it to listen to the Word of God when we pray?

My dad was very active in politics in Indiana, and he loved to discuss issues. He naturally passed on his political philosophies to me. Some of the most enjoyable times we had together were when we used to spend hours talking about political issues. What made these so enjoyable was the meeting of our minds as we talked. What I had learned from my dad through the years I was merely talking back to him. I have come to see prayer in much the same light.

Prayer is simply listening to God as He speaks to you through His Word, and then praying it back to Him—not through some formula, but as it relates to your own personal life, heartaches, needs, and aspirations. Listen to God's Word, hear what He has to say to you, and then approach Him confidently in the full assurance of faith, knowing that your prayer has been initiated by God.

5

Why Pray?

The question "Why pray?" seems to be a logical one. After all, why should we pray if God knows what we need even before we ask? Why bother if prayer isn't going to change anything anyway?

It is true that God knows our needs even before we ask, but in no way does this mean we should stop praying. The Bible not only tells us to pray, but it gives numerous reasons why. Let's take a closer look and answer the question "Why pray?"

Key Verse: John 17:3

This is eternal life: that they may know You, the only true God, and Jesus Christ, whom You have sent.

---

1. How is "eternal life" defined in this verse?

2. How do you get to know someone?

3. In what way does this verse answer the question "Why pray?"

Read Philippians 3:10,11 and answer the following questions:

1. What did Paul say he wanted out of life?

2. What power did Paul want to experience while he was here on earth? What fellowship did he want to share in?

3. What did he say the result would be in his life?

4. How does this verse answer the question "Why pray?"

God's Desire for Man

Christ died for sins once for all, the righteous for the unrighteous, to bring you to God (1 Peter 3:18).

1. Why did Christ die for sins once for all, the righteous for the unrighteous?

2. From this, what can you conclude about God's desire for man?

The former regulation is set aside because it was weak and useless (for the law made nothing perfect), and a better hope is introduced, by which we draw near to God (Hebrews 7:18,19).

1. Why was the former regulation set aside? What was introduced?

2. This better hope enables us to do what?

3. Why do you suppose God would want us to draw near to Him?

Read Romans 5:8-11 and answer the following questions:

1. How did God demonstrate His love for us?

2. Since we have been justified by His blood, what can we be confident that we will be saved from?

3. What condition were we in when we were reconciled to Christ?

4. What can we say about God's desire to have a relationship with us when we realize the costly measures He took to reconcile us to Himself?

5. It is not enough just to know about the reconciliation God provided through Jesus Christ. What does this verse say causes a person to rejoice in God?

6. Jesus Christ went to the cross so we could have a personal relationship with God as our heavenly Father. What role does prayer play in our daily relationship with God?

7. How then do these verses answer the question "Why pray?"

Knowing God's Thoughts

"My thoughts are not your thoughts, neither are your ways My ways," declares the Lord. "As the heavens are higher than the earth, so are My ways higher than your ways and My thoughts than your thoughts" (Isaiah 55:8,9).

1. According to these verses, are our thoughts and God's thoughts the same? Are our ways His ways?

2. How much higher are God's ways and thoughts than ours? How do you think we can get to know the thoughts and ways of God?

3. From these two verses how would you answer the question "Why pray?"

Read Proverbs 3:5,6 and answer the following questions:

1. According to these verses, who should we trust, and how?

2. What should we not lean on?

3. In all our ways who are we to acknowledge? How will He direct our paths?

4. Why should we pray, according to these verses?

Prayer is much like consulting the radar equipment of an airplane. The radar not only charts the course the airplane is to take but also indicates any potential danger from severe weather. With a limited scope of vision and a lack of knowledge of weather conditions, the pilot must consult and rely on his radar to avoid any danger and to guide the plane to a safe landing. So it is with prayer.

Anyone concluding that prayer is of no value is robbing himself of the greatest privilege we have as children of God. Through prayer we learn the ways of God and find His direction for our lives. What better reasons could there be to pray?

6

According to God's Will

Key Verses: 1 John 5:14,15

This is the confidence we have in approaching God: that if we ask anything according to His will, He hears us. And if we know that He hears us—whatever we ask—we know that we have what we asked of Him.

---

1. What is the confidence we have in approaching God?

2. What do you think "according to His will" means?

3. When we ask according to God's will, what can we ask for?

4. Does this mean that if we want a Cadillac, we will get it just because we have prayed and asked God for it?

5. Since we know God hears us, what else can we know?

6. What can we learn about praying according to God's will from Jesus' prayer in the Garden of Gethsemane (Matthew 26:39,42)?

We are told to pray according to God's will, but how can we know for sure what God's will is? Many of us would like to approach God with the confidence this verse describes, but we are fearful that our desires are not God's desires, so we don't pray at all.

We *can* know the will of God, however. It is not some secret that He is trying to hide from us. He wants us to know His will so that we can approach Him with confidence. Let's examine the Word of God and find out how we can know we are praying according to God's will.

What God's Will Is Not

> *As a result, he does not live the rest of his earthly life for evil human desires, but rather for the will of God. For you have spent enough time in the past doing what pagans choose to do—living in debauchery, lust, drunkenness, orgies, carousing and detestable idolatry* (1 Peter 4:2,3).

1. According to these verses, does the will of God have anything to do with gratifying evil human desires?

2. Does the will of God have anything to do with what the pagans choose to do?

3. As a matter of fact, what do these verses say about the amount of time we once spent living in debauchery, etc.?

4. Would praying according to God's will include asking God to help gratify evil human desires?

Read 1 Thessalonians 4:1-6 and answer the following questions:

1. Paul instructed the Thessalonians how to live in order to please God, and through this letter he urged them to do this more and more. What instructions did Paul give by the authority of Jesus Christ?

2. What did He say God's will is concerning sexual immorality?

3. Not only are we to avoid sexual immorality, but we are to learn to control our bodies in a way that is holy and honorable. To whom is this in direct contrast?

4. How does Paul describe the heathen?

5. What other instruction does Paul give in regard to sexual immorality?

6. The bottom line of the lifestyle of the heathen, those who do not know God and who live to gratify their lusts, is that it wrongs and takes advantage of other people. Do you see why that type of lifestyle is contrary to the will of God?

7. From this passage, what could we ask of God that would be in accordance with His will? For help in answering, focus on the words "instructed," "instructions," "learn," and "brother."

> *Do not love the world or anything in the world. If anyone loves the world, the love of the Father is not in him. For everything in the world—the cravings of sinful man, the lust of his eyes and the boasting of what he has and does—comes not from the Father but from the world. The world and its desires pass away, but the man who does the will of God lives forever* (1 John 2:15-17).

1. Why does John tell us not to love the world or anything in the world?

2. How does he describe everything in the world? Do these things come from God?

3. What is true about the world and its desires?

4. In contrast, what is true about the person who does the will of God?

5. From these verses, does the will of God sound like some secret that God is trying to hide from us, or does it sound like something we can know?

6. Does the will of God have anything to do with this world and everything in it?

7. What can we learn from these verses about praying in accordance with God's will?

How to Know God's Will

Since then you have been raised with Christ, set your hearts on things above, where Christ is seated at the right hand of God. Set your minds on things above, not on earthly things (Colossians 3:1,2).

1. Since we have been raised with Christ, where are we to set our hearts?

2. Where are we to set our minds?

3. Paul tells us not to set our minds on earthly things. Could we discern the will of God if our minds were set on these earthly things?

4. What then can we expect to discern with our hearts and minds set on things above?

> *I urge you, brothers, in view of God's mercy, to offer your bodies as living sacrifices, holy and pleasing to God—this is your spiritual act of worship. Do not conform any longer to the pattern of this world, but be transformed by the renewing of your mind. Then you will be able to test and approve what God's will is—His good, pleasing and perfect will* (Romans 12:1,2).

1. In view of God's mercy, what does Paul urge us to do?

2. What does he call it when we offer our bodies to God as a living sacrifice?

3. Paul tells us not to conform to what?

4. Based on the previous verses we have studied in this chapter, what have we learned concerning the pattern of this world?

5. In contrast, what should we do and how?

6. Through the renewing of the mind, what will we be able to discern, test, and approve?

7. According to this passage, can we know what the will of God is concerning our lives?

> *It is God who works in you to will and to act according to His good purpose* (Philippians 2:13).

1. Who is at work in us to will and to act according to God's good purpose for our lives?

2. Since God is at work in our lives to will and to act according to His good purpose, can we therefore know the will of God for our lives?

What Is His Will for My Life?

> *We are God's workmanship, created in Christ Jesus to do good works, which God prepared in advance for us to do* (Ephesians 2:10).

1. According to this verse, whose workmanship are we?

2. What were we created in Christ Jesus to do?

3. Who prepared these good works for us to do, and when?

4. From this verse, therefore, what is God's will for our lives, and in what way does this teach us to pray according to God's will?

5. In Ephesians 4:17–5:2 and Colossians 3:5-17, how does Paul define these good works that God has prepared beforehand for us to do?

6. How do these two passages compare to what we have learned about the will of God?

7. Do we have the ability to carry out these good deeds in our own strength? Who does?

8. How then should we pray, knowing that we cannot carry out these good deeds but knowing that Jesus can?

> *They asked Him, "What must we do to do the works God requires?" Jesus answered, "The work of God is this: to believe in the one He has sent"* (John 6:28,29).

1. According to Jesus, what is the work of God?

2. Could we carry out the works God has prepared for us apart from believing and depending upon Jesus Christ?

> *Remain in Me, and I will remain in you. No branch can bear fruit by itself; it must remain in the vine. Neither can you bear fruit unless you remain in Me. "I am the vine; you are the branches. If a man remains in Me and I in him, he will bear much fruit; apart from Me you can do nothing"* (John 15:4,5).

1. Can a branch bear fruit apart from the vine? How much can we do apart from Christ?

2. What is the only way we can bear fruit in our lives?

3. What then can we conclude is the will of God for us, and how does this define what praying according to God's will means?

> *In the same way, the Spirit helps us in our weakness. We do not know what we ought to pray for, but the Spirit Himself intercedes for us*

> *with groans that words cannot express. And He who searches our hearts knows the mind of the Spirit, because the Spirit intercedes for the saints in accordance with God's will. And we know that in all things God works for the good of those who love Him, who have been called according to His purpose. For those God foreknew He also predestined to be conformed to the likeness of His Son* (Romans 8:26-29).

1. When we do not know how to pray, who intercedes for us?

2. How does the Spirit intercede for the saints?

3. According to these verses, what do we know God will do for those who love Him and are called according to His purpose?

4. What is His purpose for our lives?

5. First Thessalonians 5:18 tells us what the will of God is for us—that we give thanks in all circumstances. Since God works all things together for our good, do you see why it is His will that we give thanks in all things?

6. How then do we pray according to God's will?

God has given us His Word and His Spirit to live in our hearts. It is through these two that we can know our prayers are in accordance with the will of God. He is not trying to hide His will for our lives from us. On the contrary, He has gone to great lengths to enable us to know His will and to test and approve of it and see that it is good. As we live in dependence upon Jesus and approach Him with a thankful, humble heart, we will know God's will for our lives. Then we can ask whatever we wish with the confidence that God will not only hear us but will give us whatever we ask.

7

The Attitudes of Prayer

When we communicate with God, He not only hears what we say but He also looks at the attitudes in our hearts. As 1 Samuel 16:7 says, "The Lord does not look at the things man looks at. Man looks at the outward appearance, but the Lord looks at the heart."

As we grow in our relationship with and dependence on Christ, His love begins to permeate our hearts and minds, and our attitudes begin to change. His will becomes our will, His desires become our desires, and His attitudes become our attitudes. Prayer becomes a natural response to the attitudes that He is developing in us.

Key Verse: 1 Thessalonians 5:18

Give thanks in all circumstances, for this is God's will for you in Christ Jesus.

Thanksgiving

The attitude of prayer always says "thank you." Since we know that God will cause all things to work together for our good, we can thank Him in the midst of every situation.

1. In what circumstances are we to give thanks?

2. According to this verse, what is God's will?

3. When we are giving thanks in the midst of our circumstances, who is our focus on?

4. Where is our dependence?

> *Always giving thanks to God the Father for everything, in the name of our Lord Jesus Christ* (Ephesians 5:20).

1. When we are thanking God, whose name do we do it in?

2. If we are to thank God for everything, what will our attitude continually be?

3. Why do you think it is important to be thankful?

One attitude evident in the life of Paul is a thankful heart. This attitude is not something he mustered up or included in his prayers because it sounded nice. His gratitude was in response to the grace God had extended to him in the Person of Jesus Christ. Regardless of his circumstances, Paul knew that God's grace was there for him, and that nothing could separate him from the love of God. As a result, his life overflowed with thanksgiving.

Thankfulness is the natural response to the grace of God. As a matter of fact, the Greek word for "forgive," *charis,* can be translated "the giving of thanks." A thankful heart is one of the sure signs that a person is growing in grace. As you focus on what God has done for you in the Person of Jesus Christ, your heart will naturally be filled with gratititude, and this attitude will be reflected when you pray.

Humility

He gives us more grace. That is why Scripture says: "God opposes the proud but gives grace to the humble." . . . Humble yourselves before the Lord, and He will lift you up (James 4:6,10).

1. Who is the source of all grace?

2. Can the proud heart receive God's grace?

3. How does the humble heart react to God's grace?

4. What will be the result of a humble heart before the Lord?

Humility does not come by something that we do or don't do; humility comes by simply recognizing the truth. When we see that God is everything and we are nothing, humility is a natural result.

"Has not My hand made all these things, and so they came into being?" declares the Lord. "This is the one I esteem: he who is humble and contrite in spirit, and trembles at My word" (Isaiah 66:2).

1. Does man have the power to create something from nothing?

2. Who does?

3. Who does the Lord esteem?

4. What does this verse tell us about the importance of God's Word?

5. What kind of attitude will be produced in us when we realize how awesome and powerful God is?

6. How will this affect the way we pray?

Dependence

> *I urge you, brothers, in view of God's mercy, to offer your bodies as living sacrifices, holy and pleasing to God—this is your spiritual act of worship* (Romans 12:1).

True worship is not singing or raising our hands. It involves offering our bodies as living sacrifices to God. An attitude of complete surrender to the will of God is what motivates us to pray.

1. What must we see before we can offer ourselves to God?

2. How does God's mercy motivate us to surrender ourselves to God?

3. How does God define "spiritual worship"?

4. What is significant about a living sacrifice?

> *Do not get drunk on wine, which leads to debauchery. Instead, be filled with the Spirit* (Ephesians 5:18).

An attitude of dependence is at the root of our desire to pray. Trusting Christ as our life produces in us a desire and need to communicate with the One who lives in us.

1. In light of the above verse, what are we *not* to be dependent on?

2. What does dependence on wine lead to?

3. Would you say wine has a controlling effect on someone who gets drunk?

4. What is the only thing we are to allow to control us?

5. When we are filled with the Spirit, what is the result?

Confidence

> *Faith is being sure of what we hope for and certain of what we do not see. . . . And without faith it is impossible to please God, because anyone who comes to Him must believe that He exists and that He rewards those who earnestly seek Him* (Hebrews 11:1,6).

1. How does this verse define "faith"?

2. What makes it impossible to please God?

3. Is it enough to simply believe that God exists?

4. What must we believe about God?

5. If we have faith, what can we expect when we pray?

As stated in an earlier chapter, prayer is an expression of our dependence on the Lord. He does not just help us; He *is* our very life. Therefore our dependence upon Him should be a continual, day-by-day walk of faith. Since prayer is an expression of that faith, it too should be a regular aspect of our lives. As the apostle Paul writes, "Pray without ceasing."

Our attitude of continual prayer is a result of God's love for us. Since nothing can separate us from His love, He is always there, no matter what, to communicate with us.

Pray continually (1 Thessalonians 5:17).

1. When we are praying continually, who are we in constant contact with?

2. If I am continually in communication with the Lord, who am I abiding in?

3. What is the result of abiding in Christ?

Through Jesus, therefore, let us continually offer to God a sacrifice of praise—the fruit of lips that confess His name (Hebrews 13:15).

1. Who do we go through to pray to God?

2. Why must we go through Jesus?

3. How often should we praise God?

4. According to this verse, what is the fruit of continual prayer?

5. Where is our focus when we are praising God?

Pray in the Spirit on all occasions with all kinds of prayers and requests. With this in mind, be alert and always keep on praying for all the saints (Ephesians 6:18).

To pray in the Spirit means to depend on the Holy Spirit to be the initiator of our prayers. As the Spirit speaks to our hearts about certain situations, we respond by talking to the Lord about it. As we are controlled by the Spirit, we will also pray in the Spirit.

1. In light of the above verse, in what situations are we to pray in the Spirit?

2. If we are being controlled by the Spirit, whose mind will our requests be in line with?

3. What are we to pray about?

4. Who does Paul say we are to pray for?

5. When we are praying for others, who are we not thinking of?

6. What attitude does this demonstrate?

Praying continually should not be a chore but a natural result of our dependence upon Christ. Talking and listening to the One who knows us best and loves us most is the most natural thing a peson can do. Because He knows and created everyone, He is the One we should go to in all our relationships and in all our concerns for others.

God, whom I serve with my whole heart in preaching the gospel of His Son, is my witness how constantly I remember you in my prayers at all times; and I pray that now at last by God's will the way may be opened for me to come to you (Romans 1:9,10).

1. What was the apostle Paul's main goal in life?

2. Who was his witness concerning his prayer for the people in Rome?

3. Paul had never personally met the people at the church in Rome. Yet he constantly remembered them in his prayers. What do you think he prayed for these people?

4. Paul's desire was to see these people. What would be the only way that could happen?

5. Who was Paul depending on to get him there?

As we have seen, prayer grows out of the attitudes of our heart. Thankfulness, humility, dependence, and confidence—these are the attitudes that Christ is working in us. When we are abiding in Him, His attitudes are produced in us. As a result, we have a desire to talk to God. It is the most natural thing that a Christian can do.

Are you praying to God out of a heart attitude that says "thank you"? If not, begin today to allow Christ to produce the right attitudes in and through you.

8

The Wisdom of God

Key Verses: 1 Kings 3:9-12

"Give Your servant a discerning heart to govern Your people and to distinguish between right and wrong. For who is able to govern this great people of Yours?" The Lord was pleased that Solomon had asked for this. So God said to him, "Since you have asked for this and not for long life or wealth for yourself, nor have asked for the death of your enemies but for discernment in administering justice, I will do what you have asked. I will give you a wise and discerning heart, so that there will never have been anyone like you, nor will there ever be."

1. What request did King Solomon make of God?

2. What didn't he ask for?

3. What was God's response to his request?

4. What kind of heart did God give Solomon?

As we can see from Solomon's life, his request for wisdom from God did not go unnoticed. Solomon's request showed his dependence upon God for his daily life. As we go through our own lives, we are constantly bombarded by the wisdom of this world. In order to discern truth from error, we must, like Solomon, look to God for wisdom.

As children of God we have the mind of Christ. This means we have His wisdom available to us at any time. As we walk in an attitude of dependence on His wisdom, we will begin to see life from God's perspective.

If any of you lacks wisdom, he should ask God, who gives generously to all without finding fault, and it will be given to him (James 1:5).

1. Does anybody possess all wisdom besides God?

2. Therefore, who lacks wisdom?

3. How does God give to all who ask?

4. Does He find fault with us when we go to Him in prayer?

"Who has known the mind of the Lord that he may instruct Him?"
But we have the mind of Christ (1 Corinthians 2:16).

1. What do we have as children of God?

2. Therefore, where should our wisdom come from?

3. Would it make sense for someone who has the mind of Christ to be looking to the wisdom of the world for answers?

Our source of wisdom is not in knowledge or simple understanding. True wisdom is a Person, Jesus Christ. God does not show favoritism. Anyone with Christ living in him possesses the wisdom of God, regardless of his or her educational level or mental ability.

> *It is because of Him that you are in Christ Jesus, who has become for us wisdom from God—that is, our righteousness, holiness and redemption* (1 Corinthians 1:30).

1. What has Christ Jesus become for us?

2. How is this wisdom described?

3. Who redeemed us and made us holy and righteous?

4. Who then is the focus of our wisdom?

5. In order to receive wisdom from God, who are you going to have to know?

> *My purpose is that they may be encouraged in heart and united in love, so that they may have the full riches of complete understanding, in order that they may know the mystery of God, namely, Christ, in whom are hidden all the treasures of wisdom and knowledge* (Colossians 2:2,3).

1. What was Paul's desire for his fellow Christians?

2. What will happen when we are united in love?

3. What is the mystery of God?

4. How is wisdom and knowledge from God given?

5. Therefore, are we going to trust in our own reasoning or in Christ?

One of the most misunderstood topics in the Christian life is that of spiritual warfare. The Scriptures plainly teach that we are in a spiritual battle. However, the means by which this battle is fought is many times misinterpreted. We cannot engage in any kind of "power" struggle with the enemy of our souls, for we will certainly lose. The real battle for control is in our minds. Error and lies of the enemy can only be overcome by truth. Since truth is found only in Christ, we must plug into His mind in every situation.

> *Though we live in the world, we do not wage war as the world does. The weapons we fight with are not the weapons of the world. On the contrary, they have divine power to demolish strongholds. We demolish arguments and every pretension that sets itself up against the knowledge of God, and we take captive every thought to make it obedient to Christ* (2 Corinthians 10:3-5).

1. How do we as believers wage war?

2. What are our weapons?

3. Where does this divine power come from?

4. What are some arguments that you have encountered in reference to the deity of Christ or the authority of the Bible?

5. How did you respond to those arguments?

6. Does our flesh want to naturally be obedient to Christ?

7. How do we take every thought captive?

> *If you harbor bitter envy and selfish ambition in your hearts, do not boast about it or deny the truth. Such "wisdom" does not come down from heaven but is earthly, unspiritual, of the devil. For where you have envy and selfish ambition, there you find disorder and every evil practice. But the wisdom that comes from heaven is first of all pure; then peace-loving, considerate, submissive, full of mercy and good fruit, impartial and sincere* (James 3:14-17).

1. In this passage James compares two types of wisdom—wisdom from the world and wisdom from God. Where does he say envy and selfish ambition come from?

2. When someone is envious toward another person, what is his motivation?

3. Can someone be controlled by the love of Christ and be envious at the same time?

4. What is the result of this worldly "wisdom"?

5. How is the wisdom of God described?

6. How does the wisdom of God affect our relationships with others?

The wisdom of the world is not just out in society. It can find its way into the church as well. The apostle Paul addressed this issue in the following verse:

> *Such regulations indeed have an appearance of wisdom, with their self-imposed worship, their false humility and their harsh treatment of the body, but they lack any value in restraining sensual indulgence* (Colossians 2:23).

1. What did Paul say that religious regulations have an appearance of?

2. Is this wisdom from God?

3. What do they lack?

4. What do legalistic regulations deal with, the outward or the inward?

5. Who is the only one that can deal with the heart?

The mind of Christ is the only place that we can find the wisdom of God. It is only as we depend on Him that we find guidance and direction for our lives. As we pray, we should never forget where the battle is and where the source of our victory lies. Our Father loves us unconditionally and is always there to give us wisdom and understanding through His Son, Jesus Christ.

9

What Old Testament Saints Teach Us About Prayer

___

Key Verse: Romans 15:4

For everything that was written in the past was written to teach us, so that through endurance and the encouragement of the Scriptures we might have hope.

___

1. What was the purpose of everything written in the Old Testament?

2. In your opinion, how can the Old Testament encourage us?

3. What does endurance and the encouragement of the Scriptures provide for us?

4. How will having hope affect the way we pray?

In this chapter we will examine how several Old Testament saints communicated with God. As the key verse states, the purpose in studying these saints of old is to provide hope. This is important to remember. Oftentimes, rather than being encouraged by their faith and learning we can trust the Lord with the circumstances of our lives, we try to duplicate their experiences. For example, in 1 Samuel 1 Hannah prayed for a son and the Lord gave her Samuel. The primary lesson from this story is God's faithfulness to Israel, *not* if you want a child, pray like Hannah and the Lord will answer. Trying to imitate the saints of old only leads to frustration, guilt, and failure rather than providing hope.

Also, the prayers of the Old Testament saints reflect God's purposes for the nation of Israel. The promises God made concerning forgiveness of sins and the indwelling Holy Spirit had not yet been fulfilled through the finished work of Christ. These people prayed for offspring and protection from their enemies because God chose them to be the bloodline for the coming Messiah, through whom the whole world would be blessed. They pleaded to God for mercy concerning their sins and asked that He not take His Spirit away from them because they were still looking forward to the grace that would be revealed in Christ.

Today, our prayers should reflect God's purposes for us as His children and the fact that we have been given everything we need for life and godliness in Christ Jesus. Because of the cross, our sins have been taken away and we live under a brand-new covenant. Because of Christ's resurrection, we have eternal life and are part of the body of Christ. As a result, we can pray in thankfulness for the forgiveness and life we have in Christ and that God would use us to show the world His love and grace.

With these thoughts in mind, let's take a closer look at the lives of Abraham, Moses, and David. How they communicated with God will deepen your understanding of true biblical prayer and provide hope that will enable you to approach God with confidence.

Abraham

Read Genesis 12:1-5 and answer the following questions:

1. In this conversation between God and Abram, who was doing the talking and who was doing the listening?

2. What were the specifics of God's instruction to Abram?

3. What promise did God make to Abram concerning "all peoples on earth"?

4. According to Galatians 3:16, when and through whom was this promise fulfilled?

5. Did Abram know the specifics of how God would bless all peoples through him?

6. How would you expect Abram to pray as a result?

7. The blessing of Abram comes through a personal relationship with Jesus Christ. For those in Christ, how would their prayers differ from Abram's?

8. What was Abram's response to God's instruction?

9. What can we learn from Abram's faith?

Read Genesis 15:1-6 and 17:5,17-19 and then answer the following questions:

1. What is the subject of Abraham's conversations with God in these passages?

2. How does this conversation relate back to what God had originally promised to Abraham in Genesis 12:1-5?

3. God revealed to Abraham that the world would be blessed through him. This is what Abraham talked to God about. What does this teach us about prayer?

4. How did God respond to Abraham in both Genesis 15 and 17?

5. In response to Abraham, God reaffirmed His promise and gave Abraham more detail as to how He would fulfill His promise. How did this affect Abraham's faith?

6. Can we expect answers to our prayers that will strengthen our faith and dependency upon the Lord?

7. Through his relationship with God, Abraham became "fully persuaded that God had power to do what He had promised" (Romans 4:21). What can we learn from Abraham's faith and the purpose of prayer in our lives?

Moses

Now Moses was tending the flock of Jethro his father-in-law, the priest of Midian, and he led the flock to the far side of the desert and came to Horeb, the mountain of God. There the angel of the LORD appeared to him in flames of fire from within a bush. Moses saw that though the bush was on fire it did not burn up. . . . The LORD said, "I have indeed seen the misery of My people in Egypt. I have heard them crying out because of their slave drivers, and I am concerned about their suffering. So I have come down to rescue them from the hand of the Egyptians and to bring them up out of that land into a good and spacious land, a land flowing with milk and honey—the home of the Canaanites, Hittites, Amorites, Perizzites, Hivites and Jebusites. And now the cry of the Israelites has reached Me, and I have seen the way the Egyptians are oppressing them. So now, go. I am sending you to Pharaoh to bring My people the Israelites out of Egypt." But Moses said to God, "Who am I, that I should go to Pharaoh and bring the Israelites out of Egypt?" And God said, "I will be with you. And this will be the sign to you that it is I who have sent you: When you have brought the people out of Egypt, you will worship God on this mountain" (Exodus 3:1,2,7-12).

1. Where did God appear to Moses?

2. What was God's concern for His people?

3. Because of His concern, what did God tell Moses that He had come down to do?

4. Who did God choose to lead His people out of Eygpt?

5. What was Moses' response to God?

6. With what truth did God reassure Moses?

7. From this encounter, what can we learn about God and His faithfulness to us?

Read Exodus 3:13-15 and answer the following questions:

1. What did Moses ask God in this passage?

2. Why do you suppose he asked God this question?

3. What was God's answer? What else did God say to Moses?

4. Why do you think it was important that God establish who He was to both Moses and the Israelites?

5. What does God's answer to Moses teach us about prayer?

Read Exodus 33:12-21 and answer the following questions:

1. What request did Moses make to God in verse 13?

2. Why did Moses want God to teach him His ways?

3. How did the Lord answer Moses' request?

4. Did Moses want to lead the Israelites apart from the Lord going with him?

5. What did Moses say would distinguish him and the people of God from other people on earth?

6. Today, what distinguishes the children of God from everyone else?

7. Moses was unsure that he had found favor with the Lord. What gives us the confidence as God's children that we are pleasing to Him and how will this confidence affect the way we pray in comparison to Moses?

8. What was Moses' next request to God? How did God answer Moses?

9. What does this teach us about prayer and what we will learn about God as we seek to know Him better in our own lives?

David

As a shepherd boy, David was chosen to be king of Israel. God described him as a man after His own heart. This is reflected in David's prayers, most of which are recorded in the Psalms. There, we see a man who had a very intimate relationship with God. He expressed every desire and thought of his heart, whether good or evil, to God. We can learn much from David and see that God is truly pleased with an open heart and a childlike faith that trusts Him with every circumstance of life. Let's look at a few of David's prayers and see what we can learn.

Read Psalm 51 and answer the following questions:

1. David prayed this after he committed adultery with Bathsheba. What did he ask God to do?

2. What did David know would be the only thing that could blot out his transgressions?

3. Do you think David would ask God to blot out his transgressions today knowing that Christ had died to take away our sins? How would this change David's prayer?

4. Was David depending on something he himself could do to gain forgiveness, or was he depending on the mercy of God?

5. What does his faith teach us about where our dependency needs to be?

6. David also asked God not to take His Holy Spirit away from him. This was because he had seen God take His Spirit away from Saul. According to what the Lord said in Hebrews 13:5, is this prayer applicable today for God's children?

7. In receiving God's mercy, what became David's desire concerning others?

8. If God had wanted sacrifices or burnt offerings, David said he would bring one. What did he learn were the *true* sacrifices of God?

9. What can we learn about prayer from this psalm?

> *Delight yourself in the LORD and He will give you the desires of your heart* (Psalm 37:4).

1. What does David tell us to do in this verse?

2. With what attitude should we approach God?

3. What do we have the freedom to express to God?

4. If we are delighting in the Lord, what does this verse say He will give us?

5. What can we learn from David's attitude of dependence?

Through the prayers of the Old Testament saints we can learn much about God and His character. Although they looked forward to the cross and the forgiveness that was to come, they still approached God with an attitude of dependency. They trusted Him to provide for every need and counted on Him to direct their lives so as to fulfill His purposes. And through each of their lives we see that God is indeed faithful. With this as a source of encouragement and hope, we can pray with the same attitude and heart, knowing that God will provide our every need and fulfill His purposes through us.

10

The Prayers of Paul

The apostle Paul was commissioned by God to present the grace of God in its fullness. He was sent as a missionary to the Gentiles to share the good news of "Christ in you, the hope of glory." As we read through his epistles, we can see how this revelation permeated everything he said and did.

Key Verses: Ephesians 3:16-19

I pray that out of His glorious riches He may strengthen you with power through His Spirit in your inner being, so that Christ may dwell in your hearts through faith. And I pray that you, being rooted and established in love, may have power, together with all the saints, to grasp how wide and long and high and deep is the love of Christ, and to know this love that surpasses knowledge—that you may be filled to the measure of all the fullness of God.

1. What is the first thing that Paul prays for the Ephesians? What else does he pray for them?

2. Why is it important for Christians to understand the love of God?

3. What does he mean when he says "that you may be filled to the measure of all the fullness of God"?

4. Was Paul's prayer a result of experiencing the love of God himself?

5. What can we learn from Paul's prayer for the Ephesians?

Read Ephesians 1:15-19 and answer the following questions:

1. How often did Paul pray for these people? What does that tell you about his love for them?

2. What did he ask God to give them?

3. Why did he ask God to give them the Spirit of wisdom and revelation?

4. What else did he pray for them?

5. As you read the passage, who is Paul's focus always on?

6. Was Paul praying for these people so they could *do* something or *know* something?

7. Do you think this prayer is just as applicable today as it was in Paul's day?

Read Philemon 4-7 and answer the following questions:

1. Why did Paul thank God for Philemon and remember him in his prayers?

2. What specifically did he pray for him?

3. What benefit will we receive from sharing our faith?

4. What else had Philemon done to encourage Paul?

5. What was Paul's attitude toward Philemon? Why did Paul pray for him?

6. What should motivate us to pray for other Christians?

Read Colossians 1:9-14 and answer the following questions:

1. When did Paul start praying for the Colossians? What was he asking God to fill them with?

2. Why did Paul ask God to fill the Colossians with the knowledge of His will?

3. What four things characterize a life that pleases God in every way?

4. Why did Paul pray that we be strengthened with God's power?

5. What truth enables us to joyfully give thanks to the Father?

6. What makes us qualified to share in the inheritance of the saints?

7. Was Paul's concern for us spiritual or physical?

8. How can we apply this perspective as we pray for ourselves and others?

Read Colossians 4:3,4 and answer the following questions:

1. Paul asked the Colossians to pray for him. What were his requests?

2. Being in prison at the time, what does Paul's prayer tell us about him?

3. Who was Paul depending on to open a door?

4. Could Paul do anything about his situation?

5. Why would Paul, a great apostle, ask others to pray on his behalf?

6. What does this tell us about Paul's ability and strength?

7. In the midst of your circumstances, do you see them as hopeless or as an opportunity to trust God to use them for His purpose?

Paul's dependence was not on his ability or knowledge. His faith was in the living Christ, who was alive in him and was able to do more than he could ever do in his own strength. His prayers were an expression of this dependent faith.

Paul also trusted Christ to work in the lives of other believers. His prayers for them reflect a heart of love and concern that can only come from a personal knowledge of the love of God. Just like Paul, as we talk to God about other people, He produces a love in our hearts toward them that causes us to serve and to give selflessly.

11

Making Your Requests Known to God

One of the greatest privileges we have as children of God is talking and listening to our heavenly Father. Talking to God should not be a chore but a natural result of our dependence upon Christ. Direct communication with the One who fully knows us and fully loves us is the most natural thing a child of God can do. Just as a child innocently asks his father for whatever need he may have, we can go to our heavenly Father about our relationships and needs as well as our concerns for other people.

God is never too busy to listen to our request, as small as we think it may be. He is concerned with every aspect of our lives. We can go to Him at any time and make our requests known.

Key Verses: Philippians 4:6,7

Do not be anxious about anything, but in everything, by prayer and petition, with thanksgiving, present your requests to God. And the peace of God, which transcends all understanding, will guard your hearts and your minds in Christ Jesus.

---

1. What does this passage say about being anxious?

2. Is being anxious the same thing as worrying?

3. What should we bring to God? What should our attitude be?

4. What does God promise to do when we come in this manner?

5. What does the peace of God guard in our lives in Christ Jesus?

6. Where does this put our dependence?

Cast all your anxiety on Him because He cares for you (1 Peter 5:7).

1. When you are anxious, what are you thinking about—the present or the future?

2. Can any good come from anxiety?

3. What does this verse say we are to do when we are anxious? Why can we do this?

4. How does knowing that God cares for us and always has our best in mind free us from anxiety?

5. Since God cares for you, can He be counted on to provide every need, work out every circumstance, and give you the wisdom to know what to do?

God loves us and cares for us. This is our motivation to make our requests known to Him. He may not answer like we want Him to, but there is not a better place to be than in His loving care.

Read Matthew 6:31-34 and answer the following questions:

1. When we worry about food, drink, and clothing, where is our focus?

2. Who is the true source of everything we need?

3. As children of God, what are we to be seeking after?

4. Can we count on God to meet our needs for food, shelter, and clothing?

5. In the midst of uncertainty about tomorrow, where can we find peace?

Read Matthew 7:7-11 and answer the following questions:

1. What does Jesus tell us to do? What will be the result?

2. Will God ever give us anything bad when we ask Him for something?

3. If God only gives us good things, what can you conclude about prayers not answered in the way we would like them to be?

4. If God already knows our request before we ask, why would He tell us to ask Him?

5. What does this tell you about God's view of you?

When I think of making our requests known to God, my mind flashes back to my early days as a Christian. Amy and I had received the Lord, and then we had the privilege of seeing our two children receive Christ into their hearts. As a family we grew in the love of God.

One day my daughter Debbie, who was 11 at the time, raced up to me and said, "Dad, I asked God to remove that ugly toenail and He did!" God was not obligated to answer Debbie's request, but out of a heart of love for an 11-year-old girl, God did just as she asked.

Certainly this isn't always the case. I have made numerous requests of God through the years He did not grant. This is His business, however. If He chooses not to grant a prayer request, it is because He loves us and knows what is best for our lives.

Why this one incident stands out is that here was a little girl who knew God loved her and had the power to take care of an ugly toenail. So, with a child's faith, she presented the most important request she had to her loving heavenly Father.

It was through this incident God solidified in our hearts the truth that He is interested in every detail of our lives. No matter how big or small a request may be, we have the privilege of presenting each and every one to our heavenly Father.

Pray in the Spirit on all occasions with all kinds of prayers and requests. With this in mind, be alert and always keep on praying for all the saints (Ephesians 6:18).

1. In what situations are we to pray in the Spirit?

2. If we are being controlled by the Spirit, whose mind will our requests be in line with?

3. What are we to pray about?

4. Who does Paul say we are to pray for?

5. When we are praying for others, who are we not thinking of?

6. What attitude does this demonstrate?

> *I urge, then, first of all, that requests, prayers, intercession and thanksgiving be made for everyone—for kings and all those in authority, that we may live peaceful and quiet lives in all godliness and holiness* (1 Timothy 2:1,2).

1. What did Paul urge Timothy to do?

2. What leaders should we pray for?

3. Who else?

4. Who is the focus on for changing the world's problems?

5. Why does Paul urge us to pray for our leaders?

> *God, whom I serve with my whole heart in preaching the gospel of His Son, is my witness how constantly I remember you in my prayers at all times; and I pray that now at last by God's will the way may be opened for me to come to you* (Romans 1:9,10).

1. What was Paul's one goal in life?

2. Who was his witness concerning his prayer for the people in Rome?

3. Although Paul had never met the people at the church in Rome, he constantly remembered them in his prayers. What do you think he prayed for regarding these people?

4. Paul's desire was to see these people. What would be the only way that could happen?

5. Who was he depending on to get him there?

Let's take a closer look at some specific requests that we can make known to God.

Specific Request

John 17:5,20-23 _____

Matthew 11:28 _____

2 Timothy 1:12 _____

John 8:32 _____

Luke 12:12 _____

1 Corinthians 10:13 _____

Ephesians 6:19 _____

Our requests to God should not only concern ourselves, but others as well. As we grow in the love of God, our focus becomes less inward and we begin to serve others in love. We can go to our heavenly Father with our burdens and concerns for one another.

When we see prayer as communication with a loving and attentive heavenly Father, making our requests known to Him is the most natural thing we can do. His love for us produces an attitude of dependence and trust that frees us from the bondage of fear and anxiety. When we know that He always does what is best for us, we can freely voice our concerns to Him in regard to ourselves and others.

12

Answers to Prayer

—

One thing that separates Christianity from all other religions is the fact we can have a personal relationship with God. We can know Him in an intimate way and talk to Him regularly. Knowing that God hears us when we pray, we can also conclude that He will answer our prayers. God answers our prayers according to His own will and His timing, not our own. His answer is based on what we need at a particular time. The Bible is filled with testimonies of answered prayer. Let's look at some of these and learn more about God's answers to prayer.

Key Verse: Jeremiah 33:3

Call to Me and I will answer you and tell you great and unsearchable things you do not know.

1. What is God's response when we call to Him?

2. What will He show us?

3. What does the word "unsearchable" bring to mind as you read this verse?

4. Can we figure out through our own minds what God is doing and what may be best for a given circumstance?

5. Based on this verse, should we be afraid of God's answers to our prayers?

6. What attitude does this verse indicate that we should have as we call on the Lord?

> *Every good and perfect gift is from above, coming down from the Father of the heavenly lights, who does not change like shifting shadows* (James 1:17).

1. Where does every good gift come from?

2. Where then should we look for every good and perfect gift?

3. What does James say about the character of God in this verse? Why is this significant?

4. Does it make sense to put our trust in God, since God never changes?

> *Let us then approach the throne of grace with confidence, so that we may receive mercy and find grace to help us in our time of need* (Hebrews 4:16).

1. Who is at the throne of grace?

2. What does this description tell you about God?

3. With what attitude are we to approach Him?

4. How can we have confidence in approaching God?

5. What will we receive from Him?

6. When should we approach Him?

7. According to this verse, we can be confident that we will receive grace and mercy in our time of need. Do we always know how this will spell itself out in our lives?

Many times in Scripture we see specific answers to specific prayers. There is no reason to be vague with our heavenly Father; no problem is too insignificant for Him. He loves us and wants us to depend on Him for our every need.

About midnight Paul and Silas were praying and singing hymns to God, and the other prisoners were listening to them. Suddenly there was such a violent earthquake that the foundations of the prison were shaken. At once all the prison doors flew open, and everybody's chains came loose (Acts 16:25,26).

1. Where were Paul and Silas? What were they doing?

2. What do you suppose they were praying about?

3. How did God respond?

4. Was His response immediate?

5. Can we conclude that at times God answers our prayers *yes?*

Read Acts 12:5-16 and answer the following questions:

1. Where was Peter?

2. Who was praying to God for him?

3. What happened the night before Peter was to stand trial before Herod?

4. How did Peter respond initially to what was happening?

5. After the angel had left him, what did Peter realize?

6. Where did he go?

7. What was Rhoda's response to seeing Peter?

8. When she told the others that Peter was at the door, what did they say?

9. What was their reaction when they opened the door and saw Peter standing there?

10. What does this tell you about their faith in God to answer their prayer?

11. Have you ever responded to an answered prayer in this way?

Sometimes our specific prayers are answered by God with a *no*. He knows what's best for us and what we need. The apostle Paul encountered this in the following verse. Let's see why God answered him in the negative.

Read 2 Corinthians 12:7-9 and answer the following questions:

1. What was Paul's problem?

2. Why did he have this "thorn in the flesh"?

3. What did he ask God to do? How many times did he ask God to do this?

4. What was God's response to his prayer?

5. Did God take away his problem?

6. What did Paul learn in the midst of his difficulties?

7. Could he have learned this if God had taken away his affliction?

8. What do you think God wants to teach you in the midst of your difficulties?

9. Is God more concerned about taking away our problems or teaching us to depend on Him?

We have seen through these examples that God answers yes to some prayers and no to others. There is a third answer He gives, and that is *wait*. Let's look at several passages and see why the Lord would say *wait* in answer to prayer.

It is God who works in you to will and to act according to His good purpose (Philippians 2:13).

1. Who is going to work His will in us?

2. When will God act out His good will in us?

3. Does our timing in what we ask of the Lord always coincide with His timing?

4. Do you suppose this is often the reason for delayed answers to prayer?

Your attitude should be the same as that of Christ Jesus: who, being in very nature God, did not consider equality with God something to be grasped, but made Himself nothing, taking the very nature of a servant, being made in human likeness. And being found in appearance as a man, He humbled Himself and became obedient to death—even death on a cross! (Philippians 2:5-8).

1. Whose attitude should ours be the same as?

2. What was Jesus' attitude?

3. Is your attitude always the same as that of Jesus?

4. According to these verses, why do you think God would answer to wait?

Wait for the Lord; be strong and take heart and wait for the Lord (Psalm 27:14).

1. What does David tell us to do in this passage?

2. While we wait on the Lord, what should our attitude be?

3. When we read this verse we often focus on the word "wait." But waiting can be a very frustrating experience. In what ways can this change by realizing that we are waiting *on the Lord?*

4. What kind of gifts does God give His children?

5. Therefore, should we be discouraged when we have to wait on the Lord, or should we look forward to what God is going to do in our lives?

> *To Him who is able to do immeasurably more than all we ask or imagine, according to His power that is at work within us, to Him be glory in the church and in Christ Jesus throughout all generations, for ever and ever! Amen* (Ephesians 3:20,21).

1. According to these verses, what is God able to do?

2. Where is His power at work?

3. Since it is Christ working in us, who receives the glory for our answered prayers?

There is one thing we can always be sure of: No matter how God answers our prayers, He always has our best in mind. He is a loving Father who takes care of His children. He always hears us and always answers according to His will and purpose for our lives.

13

For the Glory of God

There is no greater privilege on earth than to be a child of God and to be a part of His plan to express His love and grace to a lost and dying world. Through a thorough study of Scripture we can conclude that the chief aim of man is *to know God, to be known by God, and to make God known.* As we grow in Christ, this purpose becomes more and more apparent and will be reflected in how we pray and what we pray for. Let's take a closer look and learn what it means to pray for the glory of God.

Key Verses: John 14:13,14

I will do whatever you ask in My name, so that the Son may bring glory to the Father. You may ask Me for anything in My name, and I will do it.

1. Why did Jesus say He would do whatever we ask in His name?

2. What can we ask for in the name of Christ and be confident that He will do it?

3. According to these verses, what is the purpose of prayer?

4. In your opinion, what does it mean for the Son to bring glory to His Father?

> *No one has ever seen God, but God the One and Only, who is at the Father's side, has made Him known* (John 1:18).

1. How is the Father made known to us?

2. Could we have seen or known the Father apart from Jesus making Him known to us?

3. Through answered prayers, what do we learn about God?

When my son was ten years old I took him to a baseball game. Bobby loved baseball and couldn't wait to get to the park. He put his favorite cap on and grabbed his glove in hopes of catching a foul ball. This particular day, catching a foul ball was all Bobby could talk about. We had been to numerous games before and had never even been close to getting a foul ball. So I didn't want him to get his hopes too high and then be disappointed. Late in the game, Bobby asked if he could move down several rows to be closer to the dugout. I said sure, and off he went. As soon as he got to the dugout the batter hit a foul ball that landed right in Bobby's glove!

I'll never forget his face as he turned with ball held high in the air to say, "Look what I caught!" He came running up the bleachers with a big smile on his face. I asked him why he wanted to move down near the dugout. He said that God had told him to. You see, the most important thing to Bobby that day was catching a foul ball. God in His faithfulness to His children answered Bobby's prayer. And that day Bobby and I learned a little more of God's character and His great love for us. This is how Jesus brings glory to His Father. Through answered prayer, we are reminded how much our heavenly Father loves us and cares for us.

> *Righteous Father, though the world does not know You, I know You, and they know that You have sent Me. I have made You known to them, and will continue to make You known in order that the love You have for Me may be in them and that I Myself may be in them* (John 17:25,26).

1. As Jesus was praying to His heavenly Father, what truth did He express about the world and their knowledge of God?

2. Who truly knows the Father?

3. What did Jesus say He has done for the world and will continue doing?

4. Why does Jesus desire to continue making the Father known?

5. As children of God, in what ways do we fit into God's plan to reveal His love through Jesus Christ to the world?

6. How can this desire be reflected in the way we pray?

Read 2 Corinthians 4:4-6 and answer the following questions:

1. What has the god of this age done to the minds of unbelievers? What are they unable to see?

2. What was and is the message of Paul's preaching?

3. What did Paul say about himself?

4. What did God make shine in the heart of Paul?

5. Where do we see the glory of God?

6. How did Jesus Christ make the Father known through Paul?

7. Can He use you in the same way to make the glory of the Father known in the world today?

8. Does seeing how God used Paul create in you a desire to be used by God in the same way? If so, in what ways can you express that desire to God?

9. How will knowing that you are part of God's plan change the way you pray about the different circumstances that occur in your life?

Read 2 Corinthians 1:18-20 and answer the following questions:

1. What was the message Paul preached to the Corinthians?

2. In whom are the promises of God answered *yes?*

3. So to whose glory can we say amen if we know that every promise God made will be fulfilled through Jesus Christ?

> *This is His command: to believe in the name of His Son, Jesus Christ, and to love one another as He commanded us* (1 John 3:23).

1. What is God's command to us? How does this command show us what is truly important to God?

2. How does this affect the way we pray?

> *Whether you eat or drink or whatever you do, do it all for the glory of God* (1 Corinthians 10:31).

1. The Corinthian church argued about whether or not it was right to eat meat that had been offered to idols. What was Paul's solution to the question of whether to eat or drink, or for anything we do?

2. Earlier in 1 Corinthians 10, Paul said that everything is permissible, but not everything is beneficial. Then he said that nobody should seek his own good, but the good of others. How does this relate to doing all to the glory of God?

3. What will others learn about the love of God as you seek the good of others?

4. Do we always know what is good for others? How, then, should we pray?

Our Highest Calling

To know God, to be known by God, to make God known: This is the highest calling and the chief aim of man. We as the children of God know God, are known by God, and have the privilege of making Him known to the lost world.

It is our hope and prayer that through this study guide you will see prayer not as a means of getting what you want, but as a means of experiencing an intimate, personal relationship with Jesus Christ and an opportunity to be a part of His plan to reveal the love of the Father to a lost and dying world.

The bottom line to prayer is this: God loves you. You are His child. Talk to Him. Tell Him how you feel, tell Him about your gratitude for what He has done in your life, tell Him your needs, ask Him to fulfill your heart's desires. What He wants most from you is *you*. He wants you to grow to know Him, to love Him, and to allow Him to live through you.

Prayer is one of the greatest privileges we have as children of God. The door into His presence has been opened to us through the Person of Jesus Christ. Don't rob yourself of the opportunity to go boldly to the throne of grace, because it is there and there alone that you will find grace and mercy in your time of need.